Bill Gillham *and* Susan Hulme

Photographs by
Jan Siegieda

Methuen Children's Books

Jenny's glass is **full** . . .

but Daniel's glass is **empty**

eyes **open** . . .

and eyes **shut**

Daddy is **big** . . .

and Baby is **little**

Jenny is at the **top** of the slide . . .

and now she's at the **bottom**

Daniel is very **wet** . . .

but soon he is **dry**

Jenny climbs **over** the gate . . .

but Daniel crawls **under** it

Baby is **dirty** . . .

but now he's **clean** again

the children play **inside** . . .

and then they play **outside**

fast **asleep** . . .

and wide **awake**

Daniel is **in front** of the tree . . .

and who is **behind** it?

up and down, up and down

LET'S LOOK FOR OPPOSITES... is one of a series of four books designed to encourage children to *look* for the basic concepts of colour, shape, number and opposites in their everyday world. By talking around the topics illustrated, children will be encouraged to think of other examples and so to develop further their mastery of language and thought, quite apart from the intrinsic pleasure of sharing books with a 'helpful' adult.

Dr Bill Gillham is a well-known educational psychologist and children's author, and senior lecturer in the Department of Psychology at the University of Strathclyde.

Susan Hulme is an experienced infants' teacher, and mother of two young children, with a special interest in pre-school education.

Jan Siegieda is a freelance photographer; these are his first children's books.

*First published in Great Britain 1984
by Methuen Children's Books Ltd
11 New Fetter Lane, London EC4P 4EE
Text copyright © 1984 Bill Gillham and Susan Hulme
Photographs copyright © 1984 Bill Gillham and Jan Siegieda
Printed in Great Britain by
Hazell Watson & Viney Limited,
Member of the BPCC Group,
Aylesbury, Bucks*

ISBN 0 416 46210 3